Botpress Automation Agency: Building a 6-Figure Business From Scratch

By Silas Meadowlark

Index

- Laying the Foundation
  - Understanding Botpress and Its Capabilities
  - Defining Your Business Goals and Vision
  - Conducting Market Research and Identifying Potential Clients

- Establishing Your Botpress Automation Agency
  - Registering Your Business
  - Choosing the Right Legal Structure
  - Setting Up Your Operational Infrastructure

- Developing a Compelling Service Offering
  - Identifying In-Demand Automation Needs
  - Crafting Unique Service Packages
  - Pricing Your Services Competitively

- Building a Strong Online Presence
  - Designing an Attractive and User-Friendly Website
  - Developing a Content Marketing Strategy
  - Leveraging Social Media Platforms

- Mastering Botpress Technical Skills
  - Deepening Your Botpress Expertise
  - Staying Up-to-Date with Platform Updates
  - Optimizing Botpress Deployments

- Acquiring and Retaining Clients
  - Prospecting and Lead Generation
  - Effective Sales Strategies
  - Delivering Exceptional Customer Service

- Scaling Your Botpress Automation Agency
  - Expanding Your Team and Capabilities

- Streamlining Project Management Processes
- Exploring Automation and Outsourcing Opportunities

- Managing Finances and Profitability
  - Developing a Robust Financial Plan
  - Invoicing, Billing, and Collection Practices
  - Optimizing Costs and Maximizing Profits

- Embracing Continuous Innovation
  - Monitoring Industry Trends and Emerging Technologies
  - Experimenting with New Botpress Features
  - Adapting Your Service Offerings

- Building a Strong Brand Identity
  - Crafting a Compelling Brand Story
  - Developing a Consistent Visual Identity
  - Promoting Your Brand through Thought Leadership

- Cultivating a Talented Team
  - Recruiting and Onboarding the Right Talent
  - Fostering a Collaborative Work Culture
  - Providing Ongoing Training and Development

- Leveraging Strategic Partnerships
  - Identifying Complementary Service Providers
  - Establishing Mutually Beneficial Partnerships
  - Collaborating on Joint Projects

- Navigating Regulatory Compliance
  - Understanding Relevant Industry Regulations
  - Implementing Robust Security and Privacy Measures
  - Ensuring Ethical and Compliant Practices

- Driving Sustainable Growth
  - Diversifying Your Revenue Streams
  - Exploring International Expansion Opportunities
  - Implementing Data-Driven Decision Making

- Leaving a Lasting Legacy

- Giving Back to the Community
- Mentoring and Empowering Future Entrepreneurs
- Reflecting on Your Entrepreneurial Journey

Laying the Foundation

Understanding Botpress and Its Capabilities

Ah, Botpress - the powerful conversational AI platform that's about to remake your business. But let's be real, it's not just a plug and-play solution. Nope, to truly channel its potential, you need to dive deep, my friend. So, grab a cup of coffee (or three) and let's explore the world of Botpress together.

First things first, Botpress is more than just a chatbot builder. It's a full fledged automation powerhouse, capable of streamlining your entire business operations. From lead generation to customer support, Botpress can handle it all. And the best part? It's open source, which means you have the freedom to customize it to your heart's content.

But don't just take my word for it. Botpress is packed with features that'll make your life easier, like natural language understanding, sentiment analysis, and even multi language support. And the cherry on top? It's built on Node.js, so if you're a JavaScript aficionado, you'll feel right at home.

Now, I know what you're thinking: "But how do I actually put all this power to use?" Well, buckle up, because the possibilities are endless. Botpress can automate your lead capture, handle customer inquiries, and even schedule appointments. And let's not forget about the power of integrations – with Botpress, you can connect to your favorite tools and create a uninterrupted, end to-end workflow.

So, what are you waiting for? Dive in, explore, and let Botpress let loose its magic on your business. Trust me, once you see what it can do, you'll be wondering how you ever lived without it.

Defining Your Business Goals and Vision

Alright, now that you've got a handle on Botpress and its capabilities, it's time to get serious about your business goals and vision. Because let's be real, without a clear direction, you might as well be wandering the desert, hoping to stumble upon an oasis of success.

First things first, take a step back and ask yourself: What do I want to achieve with my Botpress automation agency? Do I want to be the go to provider for small businesses in my local area? Or maybe I dream of building a global powerhouse, serving clients worldwide? Whatever your vision, it's important to have it crystal clear in your mind.

But don't just stop there. Break down those big, hairy, audacious goals into bite sized, doable steps. Maybe your first milestone is to land your first client, or maybe it's to build a team of top notch Botpress experts. Whatever it is, make sure it's measurable, achievable, and most importantly, matched with your overall vision.

And let's not forget about the financial side of things. What kind of revenue and profitability targets are you aiming for? Are you looking to build a lifestyle business, or do you want to scale up and create something truly massive? Again, be specific, and don't be afraid to dream big. After all, this is your chance to shape the future of your agency.

Remember, your goals and vision are the foundation upon which your entire Botpress automation agency will be built. So take the time to really think them through, and don't be afraid to adjust course as you go. Because trust me, the journey ahead is full of surprises, and having a clear North Star will be your guiding light.

Conducting Market Research and Identifying Potential Clients

Alright, time to put on your detective hat and dive into the world of market research. Because let's be honest, you can't just wing it and hope for the best when it comes to building a successful Botpress automation agency. Nope, you need to know your target market like the back of your hand.

First up, let's talk about identifying your potential clients. Now, I know what you're thinking - "But I want to work with everyone!" - but trust me, that's a surefire way to end up spread too thin. Instead, focus on a specific niche or industry where you can truly shine.

Maybe it's small and medium sized e commerce businesses that need help streamlining their customer service. Or perhaps you're the go to expert for tech startups looking to automate their sales and marketing processes. Whatever it is, make sure it coordinates with your unique strengths and the is a problem you're best equipped to solve.

But don't just take my word for it. Get out there and start talking to your potential clients. Ask them about their biggest challenges, their current solutions, and what they're looking for in a Botpress automation partner. This kind of first hand insight is pure gold, my friend, and it'll help you craft a service offering that's tailor made for their needs.

And let's not forget about the competition. Who else is out there serving your target market? What are they doing well, and where are the gaps you can fill? Analyze their pricing, their service products, and their marketing strategies. This intel will not only help you differentiate yourself, but it'll also give you a leg up in the battle for client attention.

Remember, market research isn't a one and-done deal. It's an ongoing process that should inform every aspect of your Botpress automation agency, from your service packages to your pricing and beyond. So dive in, get your hands dirty, and let the data be your guide to building a thriving, future proof business.

Establishing Your Botpress Automation Agency

Registering Your Business

So, you've taken the plunge and decided to launch your very own Botpress Automation Agency. Buckle up, my friend, because this is where the real adventure begins. First things first: let's get your business officially registered and ready to take on the world.

Now, I know what you're thinking - bureaucratic red tape and endless paperwork, right? Fear not, my entrepreneurial comrade, for I come bearing the secrets to navigating this process with the grace and finesse of a seasoned cat burglar. Just follow my lead, and you'll be strutting into that government office like you own the place.

The key is to approach this step with the same level of enthusiasm you'd have for a root canal. Feign interest, make small talk with the clerk about their favorite brand of paper clips, and you'll have that business license in your hands before you can say "tax deduction." And don't forget to throw in a few spontaneous dance moves for good measure - nothing says "trustworthy business owner" like a killer robot impression.

Once you've got that all important piece of paper in your possession, it's time to start laying the groundwork for your Botpress empire. Remember, this is your chance to create the ultimate superhero lair, complete with a secret entrance, a high tech command center, and a fully stocked snack bar. Okay, maybe not the secret entrance, but the rest is totally doable.

Choosing the Right Legal Structure

Now that your business is officially registered, it's time to make another critical decision: choosing the right legal structure. This is where things can get a little tricky, like navigating a minefield of tax codes and legalese, but fear not – I've got your back.

First, let's address the elephant in the room: sole proprietorship or limited liability company (LLC)? It's like choosing between a plain ol' PB&J or a triple decker bacon wrapped, deep fried masterpiece. Sure, the PB&J may be the safer option, but where's the fun in that? Go big or go home, I always say.

Now, I know what you're thinking – "But what about the liability? Won't I be risking my firstborn child and my entire life savings?" Well, my friend, that's where the LLC comes in. It's like a superhero cape for your business, shielding you from the risks of the world (and angry clients who didn't appreciate your bot's interpretive dance routine).

But don't just take my word for it. Gather your closest confidants, pour a glass of your finest sparkling water, and engage in a good old fashioned pros and cons list session. And don't be afraid to think outside the box – maybe you're the type who thrives in a general partnership, or perhaps you're feeling bold and want to explore the world of cooperative ownership. The possibilities are endless, my friend, so let your creativity run wild!

Setting Up Your Operational Infrastructure

Alright, now that you've got your business all registered and your legal structure in place, it's time to start building the foundation for your Botpress Automation Agency. Think of this as the behind the-scenes magic that will make your agency hum like a well oiled machine - or, you know, a bot that's been properly calibrated.

First and foremost, you'll need to set up your office space. Now, I know what you're thinking - "Boring! I'd rather be tinkering with my bot's dance moves." But trust me, a well designed workspace can be the difference between productivity and pure chaos. So, channel your inner interior designer and create a space that's equal parts functionality and flair.

Next up, let's talk about your tech stack. This is where you get to indulge your inner tech geek and play with all the shiny new toys. From project management tools to cloud based storage solutions, the options are endless. Just remember, the key is to find a balance between efficiency and the latest and greatest - you don't want to end up with a tech graveyard, after all.

And last but not least, let's not forget about the all important task of hiring your dream team. After all, what's a Botpress Automation Agency without a group of talented individuals who can bring your bot tastic visions to life? So, start scouring the job boards, networking like a boss, and keep your eyes peeled for those hidden gems who can take your agency to new heights.

Developing a Compelling Service Offering

Identifying In Demand Automation Needs

Ah, the sweet spot where automation meets customer demand - that's the holy grail for any Botpress Automation Agency worth its salt. But how do you find that elusive intersection? It's all about digging deep, my friend. Start by putting on your detective hat and scouring the market for the is a challenge that keep your potential clients up at night.

Don't just settle for surface level information. Dive into industry forums, social media, and good old fashioned one on-one conversations. Listen for the frustrated cries of "If only there was a way to..." or the desperate pleas of "I can't keep up with all this manual work!" Those, my friends, are the golden tickets that will lead you to automation nirvana.

Once you've amassed a rich source of perceptions, it's time to get strategic. Analyze the data, spot the patterns, and identify the automation sweet spots that harmonize with your agency's capabilities. Are there certain tasks or workflows that your Botpress expertise can rationalize with lightning fast efficiency? Lean into those opportunities and let your potential clients know that you've got the perfect solution to their problems.

Remember, the key is to position your agency as the indispensable partner that can transform chaos into order, freeing up your clients to focus on the high value, needle moving activities that truly drive their business forward. Become the automation whisperer they never knew they needed, and watch your client roster swell with eager businesses ready to embrace the Botpress revolution.

Crafting Unique Service Packages

Now that you've identified the automation needs that are keeping your potential clients up at night, it's time to work your magic and craft those irresistible service packages. But hold on, this isn't your run of-the mill, one size-fits all approach. No, sir, this is where you get to flex your creative muscles and show the world that your Botpress Automation Agency is anything but ordinary.

Start by thinking outside the box. Sure, you could offer the standard "Botpress for Beginners" package, but where's the fun in that? Instead, why not create a "Botpress Bootcamp" that immerses your clients in the world of conversational AI, complete with hands on workshops and a personalized roadmap to automation domination?

Or how about a "Botpress Blitz" package that promises lightning fast deployments and rapid ROI? Imagine the look on your clients' faces when you tell them you can have their dream chatbot up and running in a matter of days, not weeks. It's the kind of service that will have them scrambling to sign on the dotted line before you can even finish your pitch.

And let's not forget the power of customization. Sure, you can have your standard service options, but be prepared to flex your creative muscles and tailor your solutions to each client's unique needs. After all, when it comes to automation, one size definitely doesn't fit all. Show your clients that you're willing to go the extra mile, and they'll be more than happy to entrust their Botpress dreams to your capable hands.

Pricing Your Services Competitively

Ah, the age old question that haunts every entrepreneur: how the heck do you price your services? It's a delicate dance, my friends, but fear not – with a little bit of strategic thinking and a dash of creative flair, you can nail the perfect pricing structure for your Botpress Automation Agency.

First and foremost, forget about hourly rates. That's so 20th century. Instead, let's get creative and start thinking in terms of value based pricing. What's the true impact your Botpress solutions can have on your clients' businesses? Are we talking about shaving hours off their workflow, boosting engagement by 50%, or freeing up their team to focus on more strategic initiatives? Those are the metrics that matter, and that's what you need to be pricing for.

Now, don't be afraid to get a little quirky with your pricing models. Why not offer a "Botpress Blitz" package that guarantees a lightning fast deployment, complete with a "coffee spit" scale that charges extra for every time your work makes a client do a spit take? Or how about a "Botpress Mastery" program that includes personalized coaching and a VIP hotline for those oh so-critical tech support emergencies?

And let's not forget the power of bundling. By packaging your services in a way that speaks to your clients' needs, you can not only optimize your options but also create a sense of irresistible value. Imagine a "Botpress Automation Suite" that includes everything from custom chatbot development to in depth analytics and reporting – it's the kind of comprehensive solution that'll have your clients singing your praises from the rooftops.

Remember, the key to pricing your Botpress Automation Agency's services is to strike the perfect balance between profitability and perceived value. Price too low, and you risk devaluing your expertise; price too high, and you might scare off potential clients. So, keep a keen eye on the market, stay attuned to your clients' needs, and don't be afraid to get a little creative. After all, when it comes to building a thriving Botpress Automation Agency, thinking outside the box is just part of the job description.

Building a Strong Online Presence

Designing an Attractive and User Friendly Website

In the digital age, your website is the heart and soul of your Botpress Automation Agency. It's the first impression potential clients will have of your business, so it's critical to get it right. Forget about those cookie cutter templates - you need a website that screams "unique, new, and totally worth your time."

Start by ditching the boring corporate look and embrace a bold, visually striking design. Think eye catching graphics, vibrant color schemes, and a layout that's as intuitive as a toddler navigating an iPad. Remember, you're not just selling your services; you're selling a vibe, an experience. So make sure every pixel on that screen exudes the same level of creativity and personality that your team brings to the table.

But don't stop there. Usability is key. Your website should be a fluid, frictionless journey for your visitors, guiding them effortlessly from that eye catching homepage to the oh so-irresistible call to-action. Implement smart navigation, sleek animations, and a search function that puts Google to shame. After all, the last thing you want is for a potential client to get lost in the digital wilderness, only to emerge frustrated and head straight to your competition.

Developing a Content Marketing Strategy

Once you've got the website sorted, it's time to start building your online presence through the power of content. But not just any content - we're talking about the kind of stuff that makes your audience sit up, take notice, and say, "Whoa, these guys really know their stuff."

Begin by identifying your brand's unique voice and personality. Are you the witty, sarcastic sidekick, always ready with a perfectly timed quip? Or perhaps you're the wise, sage like mentor, offering understanding that will forever change the way your readers think about Botpress automation. Whichever route you choose, make sure it coordinates seamlessly with your overall brand identity.

Next, create a content calendar that's as dynamic and unpredictable as a toddler on a sugar high. Mix up your formats - blog posts, webinars, video tutorials, infographics, the works. And don't be afraid to get a little weird. Who says your Botpress tips can't be delivered through the medium of interpretive dance? The key is to keep your audience engaged, entertained, and always coming back for more.

Remember, content marketing is a long game, not a quick sprint. Consistency is key, but don't be afraid to experiment, adjust, and find new ways to connect with your target audience. After all, the digital scene is ever evolving, and the true masters of the craft are the ones who can adapt and thrive in the face of change.

Leveraging Social Media

Platforms

In the wild, wild world of digital marketing, social media is the untamed frontier - a place where the bold and the brave can rise to greatness, or crash and burn in a flaming heap of emojis and hastags. But fear not, my fellow Botpress aficionados, for with the right strategy, you can tame these social media beasts and turn them into your most powerful allies.

First and foremost, choose your platforms wisely. Don't try to be everywhere at once - that's a surefire recipe for burnout and a seriously neglected Instagram account. Instead, focus on the networks where your target audience is most active and engaged. Maybe that's LinkedIn for the corporate crowd, or TikTok for the Gen Z trendsetters. Heck, maybe it's a niche forum dedicated to the art of interpretive Botpress dance. The key is to meet your people where they're at.

Once you've settled on your channels, it's time to get creative. Forget about the standard "look at us, we're so professional" posts. Instead, embrace the weird, the wacky, and the wonderfully unexpected. Post behind the-scenes glimpses of your team's shenanigans, host impromptu Q&A sessions, or launch a social media campaign that has everyone scratching their heads and wondering, "Wait, is this for real?"

And let's not forget the power of influencer marketing. Forget about those cookie cutter influencers with millions of followers - the true magic happens when you partner with niche is an expert, industry experts, and quirky personalities who can help you reach your ideal clients in a way that feels genuine and authentic. After all, in the age of social media, trust is the new currency, and you've got to be willing to think outside the box to earn it.

Mastering Botpress Technical Skills

Deepening Your Botpress Expertise

If you want to build a thriving Botpress automation agency, you need to be more than just a casual user of the platform. It's time to dive deep and become a true Botpress virtuoso. Sure, you might have picked up the basics during the earlier stages of your entrepreneurial journey, but now it's time to take your skills to the next level.

First and foremost, immerse yourself in the Botpress documentation. Don't just skim through it - study it like a medieval monk poring over ancient tomes. Familiarize yourself with the intricacies of the platform, from the core architecture to the advanced features that can give your clients the "wow" factor they crave. Experiment relentlessly, pushing the boundaries of what Botpress can do.

But don't stop there. Engage with the Botpress community, both online and in real life. Attend local meetups, join forums, and connect with other Botpress enthusiasts. The collective wisdom and shared experiences of this vibrant community can be an priceless asset as you navigate the ever evolving scene of conversational AI.

And let's not forget about certifications. Pursue Botpress specific training and earn those shiny badges of honor. Not only will this improve your credibility, but it will also deepen your understanding of the platform, ensuring that you're always one step ahead of the competition.

Staying Up to-Date with Platform Updates

In the world of technology, change is the only constant. And when it comes to Botpress, you can bet that the platform is constantly evolving, with new features, updates, and improvements being rolled out on a regular basis. As a savvy Botpress automation agency, it's your job to stay on top of these developments, ensuring that you're always offering your clients the latest and greatest capabilities.

Set aside time each week to review the Botpress release notes, scour the community forums for updates, and keep an eye on the Botpress blog. This way, you'll be the first to know about any game changing features or enhancements that could give your agency a competitive edge.

But it's not just about reading release notes – you need to put these updates into practice. Regularly test new Botpress features and functionalities, experimenting with them in your own projects before introducing them to your clients. This hands on approach will not only deepen your understanding but also help you identify any potential pitfalls or limitations that could impact your client's deployments.

By staying ahead of the curve, you'll be able to provide your clients with cutting edge solutions that keep them ahead of the competition. Plus, you'll earn a reputation as the Botpress automation agency that's always on the pulse of the latest industry trends and innovations.

Optimizing Botpress Deployments

As your Botpress automation agency grows, you'll find yourself managing an increasingly complex system of client deployments. And with great power comes great responsibility – it's up to you to ensure that each and every one of those deployments is running at peak efficiency.

Start by developing a comprehensive Botpress deployment playbook. This should include effective techniques for infrastructure setup, configuration management, scaling, monitoring, and troubleshooting. Invest in the right tools and platforms to automate and simplify these processes, freeing up your team to focus on more strategic initiatives.

But optimization isn't just about the technical side – it's also about optimizing the user experience. Work closely with your clients to understand their is a problem, pain thresholds, and desired outcomes. Then, use Botpress's powerful analytics and reporting capabilities to fine tune your deployments, ensuring that your clients are getting the maximum value from their investment.

And let's not forget the importance of ongoing maintenance and support. Establish clear SLAs with your clients, outlining your response times, issue resolution processes, and continuous improvement strategies. This will not only keep your clients happy but also solidify your reputation as a reliable and trustworthy Botpress automation partner.

Acquiring and Retaining Clients

Prospecting and Lead Generation

Forget the days of cold calling and mass emails - in the high octane world of Botpress automation, we're talking about prospecting with a twist. Ditch the generic pitch and embrace your inner showman. When it comes to landing those dream clients, the name of the game is strategic serendipity.

Start by diving deep into the world of your target audience. Become a veritable stalker - I mean, an expert researcher - scouring the internet for clues about their is a difficulty, their goals, and their secret desires. Once you've cracked the code, it's time to get creative.

Surprise and delight your prospects with personalized gifts that showcase your ingenuity. Send them a custom made bot that answers all their burning questions, or a quirky video that leaves them chuckling and intrigued. The key is to stand out from the crowd and make them feel like you're speaking directly to their needs.

And don't be afraid to get a little...unconventional. Host a virtual game night with your potential clients, where the prize is a free consultation. Or organize a themed scavenger hunt that leads them straight to your door (or, you know, your virtual inbox).

Remember, success in this game is all about building genuine connections. Treat your prospects like long lost friends, and they'll be more likely to see you as a trusted partner, not just another vendor vying for their attention.

Effective Sales Strategies

Forget the hard sell, folks. In the world of Botpress automation, the real magic happens when you ditch the script and embrace your inner storyteller. Sure, you could bombard your clients with a laundry list of features and benefits, but why not take them on a journey instead?

Start by understanding their unique challenges and painting a vivid picture of how your Botpress solutions can transform their business. Weave in real life success stories, sprinkle in a dash of humor, and watch as they become captivated by the possibilities.

But don't stop there. Engage your prospects in a collaborative dialogue, inviting them to share their thoughts and ideas. After all, the best partnerships are those where both parties feel invested in the outcome.

And when it comes to closing the deal, forget the hard nosed negotiation tactics. Instead, focus on creating a sense of mutual value and trust. Offer flexible pricing options, personalized service packages, and a commitment to their long term success. Remember, you're not just selling a product – you're building a relationship that will stand the test of time.

Delivering Exceptional

Customer Service

In the world of Botpress automation, client satisfaction isn't just a box to check - it's the very foundation of your success. And that means going above and beyond the standard customer service playbook.

Start by cultivating a deep understanding of your clients' unique needs and is a difficulty. Anticipate their questions before they even arise, and be ready to offer tailored solutions that address their challenges head on. Become a true partner in their success, not just a vendor they call when things go wrong.

But it's not just about technical expertise - it's about the human touch. Infuse every interaction with a genuine sense of warmth and care. Remember their birthdays, send handwritten notes, and genuinely celebrate their victories. After all, in the high stakes world of Botpress automation, it's the little things that can make all the difference.

And when the inevitable hiccups do occur, don't just offer a standard apology - turn it into an opportunity to showcase your commitment. Respond swiftly, take ownership of the issue, and work tirelessly to find a resolution that exceeds their expectations. Remember, the true measure of your service isn't how you handle the easy stuff - it's how you handle the curveballs.

So, forget the one size-fits all approach. Tailor your customer service to the unique needs of each client, and watch as they become raving fans, singing your praises from the rooftops (or, you know, their social media platforms).

Scaling Your Botpress Automation Agency

Expanding Your Team and Capabilities

As your Botpress Automation Agency starts to gain traction and your client base grows, it's time to consider expanding your team and capabilities. After all, you can't be a one person bot wrangling wonder forever. The key is to build a dynamic, adaptable workforce that can keep up with the ever evolving demands of your clients.

Begin by taking a hard look at your current skill set and where the gaps lie. Do you need a Botpress wizard who can work their magic on complex integrations? A social media savant to manage your clients' online presence? Or perhaps a data analyst to crunch the numbers and uncover those hidden understanding? Whatever your needs, make sure to hire people who complement your own strengths and bring something unique to the table.

But hiring isn't just about finding the right talent – it's also about creating a collaborative, enabled work culture. Encourage your team to share their ideas, challenge the status quo, and constantly push the boundaries of what's possible with Botpress. After all, the best innovations often come from the minds of those who aren't afraid to color outside the lines.

As your team grows, so too should your agency's capabilities. Invest in ongoing training and development, staying on top of the latest Botpress updates and standards. Attend industry events, participate in online communities, and continually expand your knowledge. The more versatile and well rounded your team becomes, the more value you can bring to your clients.

Streamlining Project Management Processes

With a thriving Botpress Automation Agency comes the inevitable challenge of managing an increasingly complex portfolio of projects and clients. It's time to level up your project management game, folks. No more sticky notes and back of-the napkin scribbles – it's time to set in motion the power of organized chaos.

First and foremost, establish a centralized project management system that brings all your client work under one digital roof. Explore project management tools like Asana, Trello, or Basecamp, and find the one that best fits your agency's workflow. These platforms will help you track tasks, deadlines, and team collaboration with laser like precision, keeping everyone on the same page (and out of each other's hair).

Speaking of your team, enable them to take ownership of their own projects. Encourage a culture of transparency and accountability, where everyone knows what they're responsible for and can proactively address any roadblocks. Regular check ins, team retrospectives, and clear communication will be the glue that holds your agency together as it continues to grow.

And let's not forget the all important client communication.

Implement a streamlined process for keeping your clients in the loop, whether it's through weekly status updates, milestone reviews, or real time access to project dashboards. The more visibility you can provide, the more trust and confidence you'll build with your clients – and the more likely they'll be to stick around for the long haul.

Exploring Automation and Outsourcing Opportunities

As your Botpress Automation Agency matures, it's time to start thinking about ways to employ automation and outsourcing to drive greater efficiency and scalability. After all, you can only clone yourself so many times before the mad scientist look starts to become a liability.

First up, let's talk about automating those repetitive, time consuming tasks that are slowly draining the life force from your team. Botpress is, well, your bot powered secret weapon. Use the platform's powerful integration capabilities to automate everything from client onboarding and progress reporting to data analysis and email marketing. The more you can offload to your trusty bot army, the more headspace your team will have to focus on high value, strategic work.

But automation isn't the only trick up your sleeve. Consider strategically outsourcing certain functions to specialized providers, freeing up your internal resources for core competencies. Maybe you partner with a virtual assistant service to handle administrative tasks, or collaborate with a content creation agency to produce top notch thought leadership pieces. The key is to identify the areas where you can make use of external expertise to drive greater efficiency and profitability.

Of course, with any outsourcing or automation initiative, you'll want to maintain a watchful eye on quality control and client satisfaction. Develop vigorous processes for vetting partners, managing handoffs, and ensuring a uninterrupted experience for your clients. After all, the last thing you want is for your bot army to stage a coup and leave your clients high and dry.

Managing Finances and Profitability

Developing a Powerful Financial Plan

Running a successful Botpress automation agency isn't just about creating dazzling chatbots and automating all the things - it's also about keeping a close eye on your financial well being. Sure, you could wing it and hope for the best, but trust me, that's a one way ticket to a world of hurt. No, my friends, the key to long term prosperity is a solid financial plan that'll make even the most seasoned bean counter swoon.

Start by taking a long, hard look at your business goals and projections. Where do you see your agency in the next 3, 5, even 10 years? Use that crystal ball of yours to map out a financial roadmap that'll get you there. Factor in everything from startup costs and ongoing operational expenses to anticipated revenue streams and potential growth opportunities.

But don't stop there - this ain't your average spreadsheet. Weave in a healthy dose of contingency planning, because let's face it, life has a way of throwing curveballs when you least expect it. Build in some wiggle room to handle unexpected challenges, whether it's a bot glitch that sends your support team into a tailspin or a global pandemic that turns your client base upside down.

And speaking of clients, make sure your financial plan

accounts for their payment habits and potential delinquencies. Trust me, nothing ruins a good mood like chasing down overdue invoices. Set up a streamlined invoicing and collection system, and don't be afraid to get creative with incentives or consequences to keep those payments flowing.

Remember, your financial plan isn't just a static document - it's a living, breathing blueprint that should evolve alongside your agency. Review it regularly, make adjustments as needed, and don't be afraid to get a second opinion from a savvy financial advisor. After all, the key to building a truly sustainable Botpress automation agency is having a financial foundation that's as rock solid as the bots you deploy.

Invoicing, Billing, and Collection Practices

Ah, the sweet sound of cha ching - or is it the soul crushing silence of unpaid invoices? As the mastermind behind your Botpress automation agency, it's up to you to ensure that the money's flowing in as smoothly as your bots are flowing out.

Start by setting up a streamlined invoicing system that'll make your clients' eyes light up with joy (or at least not cause them to groan in despair). Invest in a user friendly invoicing platform that integrates seamlessly with your accounting software, making it a breeze to track payments, generate detailed reports, and follow up on overdue bills.

But invoicing is just the tip of the iceberg. You'll also need to develop a clear and transparent billing structure that leaves no room for confusion or surprises. Break down your services into easily understandable line items, and be upfront about any additional fees or charges. After all, nothing kills the mood quite like a client getting blindsided by a hidden 'chatbot maintenance' surcharge.

And when it comes to collection practices, you'll want to strike the perfect balance between being firm and being friendly. Start with gentle reminders, but don't be afraid to get a little more assertive if the payment keeps dragging on. Maybe even offer a 'pay on-time' discount to stimulate prompt payments. Just be sure to stay professional, even when the client is being, well, less than ideal.

Remember, your invoicing, billing, and collection practices are a direct reflection of your agency's brand and credibility. So why not have a little fun with it? Slip in a quirky joke or two in your email reminders, or offer a 'bot themed' discount for clients who pay in Bitcoin (you know, for the crypto savvy crowd).

At the end of the day, keeping your agency's cash flow healthy is vital for your long term success. So embrace your inner finance guru, get creative with your billing strategies, and watch those invoices roll in like a well oiled machine.

Optimizing Costs and Maximizing Profits

Ah, the holy grail of running a Botpress automation agency: maximizing your profits while keeping those pesky costs in check. It's a delicate balancing act, to be sure, but with the right strategies in your arsenal, you can turn your agency into a veritable cash cow.

Start by taking a detailed examination into your operational expenses. Scrutinize every line item, from your Botpress hosting fees to the monthly coffee tab for the team. Identify any areas where you can trim the fat, whether it's negotiating better deals with vendors or finding more cost effective alternatives for your tech stack.

But don't stop there - it's time to get creative with revenue boosting tactics. Experiment with different pricing models, such as tiered service packages or pay per-use pricing. Heck, you could even offer a 'bot of-the month' subscription service for clients who want to stay on the cutting edge of Botpress technology.

And let's not forget about the power of upselling and cross selling. Keep a close eye on your client's needs and is an issue, and be ready to introduce them to new Botpress powered solutions that can take their business to the next level. After all, who doesn't love the idea of a chatbot that can also do their taxes?

Of course, none of this matters if you can't keep your clients happy and coming back for more. Invest in exceptional customer service, go the extra mile to ensure their satisfaction, and watch as those repeat business and referrals start pouring in. After all, happy clients mean happier bank balances for you.

Remember, the key to maximizing your Botpress automation agency's profitability isn't just about cutting costs and jacking up prices. It's about finding the perfect balance between efficiency, innovation, and customer delight. So roll up your sleeves, get creative, and watch those profits soar to dizzying new heights.

Embracing Continuous Innovation

Monitoring Industry Trends and Emerging Technologies

In the rapidly evolving world of digital automation, standing still is simply not an option. To stay ahead of the curve and maintain a competitive edge, your Botpress Automation Agency must be a unceasing seeker of knowledge - constantly scanning the horizon for the next big thing. Sure, you could hunker down and focus solely on perfecting your current suite of services, but that's a surefire way to find yourself quickly outpaced by the industry's trailblazers.

So, how do you keep your finger on the pulse of the Botpress network and the broader automation terrain? First and foremost, immerse yourself in the community. Attend industry events, both virtual and in person, where you can rub elbows with the innovators and visionaries shaping the future. Engage with online forums, Slack channels, and social media groups, soaking up the understanding and experiences of your peers. The more you connect with the movers and shakers in the space, the better equipped you'll be to anticipate the next big shift.

But don't just rely on others to keep you informed - become a voracious consumer of industry publications, blogs, and thought leadership content. Scour the web for the latest news, case studies, and expert analyses, and make a habit of regularly reviewing Botpress' own roadmap and feature updates. By constantly expanding your knowledge and staying attuned to the zeitgeist, you'll be poised to identify emerging opportunities and change direction your service selections accordingly.

Remember, the true power of continuous innovation lies in your ability to quickly and seamlessly adapt to change. So, embrace a mindset of flexibility and agility, and be ready to experiment and iterate at a moment's notice. After all, the only constant in this industry is change, and the agencies that thrive are the ones that aren't afraid to get a little bit messy in the pursuit of progress.

Experimenting with New Botpress Features

As the saying goes, "the only way to truly learn is by doing." And when it comes to staying on the cutting edge of Botpress, that couldn't be more true. Sure, you can read all the documentation and attend all the webinars, but until you roll up your sleeves and get your hands dirty, you'll never fully open up the power of this dynamic platform.

That's why it's so important to promote a culture of experimentation within your Botpress Automation Agency. Carve out dedicated time and resources for your team to explore new Botpress features, tinker with various configurations, and push the boundaries of what's possible. Encourage them to think outside the box, to dream up wild and unconventional use cases, and to embrace the thrill of the unknown.

And when those experiments inevitably lead to a few bumps in the road, don't view it as a failure - see it as an opportunity to learn and grow. Dissect what went wrong, analyze the lessons learned, and use that knowledge to refine your approach. After all, the true measure of innovation isn't a flawless final product, but rather the journey of trial and error that got you there.

By authorizing your team to be bold, curious, and unafraid of making mistakes, you'll nurture a culture of continuous improvement that will ripple through every aspect of your Botpress Automation Agency. Your clients will be the ones who reap the rewards, as you deliver increasingly sophisticated and inventive solutions that keep them one step ahead of the competition.

Adapting Your Service Services

In the ever evolving world of Botpress and digital automation, the only constant is change. And as a forward thinking Botpress Automation Agency, it's your responsibility to stay ahead of the curve, anticipating the needs of your clients and adapting your service selections accordingly.

Begin by closely monitoring the trends and shifts within your target industries. Keep a keen eye on the is a difficulty your clients are facing, the emerging technologies they're exploring, and the evolving regulatory scene they're navigating. By staying attuned to their changing needs, you'll be able to proactively develop new services and solutions that address their most pressing concerns.

But don't just focus on reacting to the market - take a more proactive approach by actively shaping the future of your industry. Apply your deep Botpress expertise and your novel mindset to identify untapped opportunities and unmet demands. Experiment with new service models, explore bold and unconventional ideas, and be willing to take calculated risks in pursuit of game changing solutions.

Remember, the key to maintaining a competitive edge is to never become complacent. Continuously assess your service portfolio, identify areas for improvement, and seek out new avenues for growth. Collaborate with your clients, solicit their feedback, and use those understanding to inform your product roadmap. By remaining adaptable, responsive, and hyper focused on delivering maximum value, you'll position your Botpress Automation Agency as the indispensable partner of choice for businesses seeking to employ the power of digital automation.

Building a Strong Brand Identity

Crafting a Compelling Brand Story

Ah, the sweet aroma of a freshly brewed cup of brand identity. It's the secret sauce that sets your Botpress Automation Agency apart from the sea of generic providers out there. But don't worry, we're not talking about some stuffy, corporate mumbo jumbo. No, my friend, we're going to craft a brand story that's as unique and captivating as a Shakespearean sonnet – with a twist of good old fashioned quirkiness, of course.

First things first, let's ditch the boring "About Us" page and get personal. Your brand story is the heartbeat of your agency, so why not let it shine with a little of your own personality? Think of it as an open invitation for your clients to get to know the real you – the one who's not afraid to wear mismatched socks and break out in a spontaneous interpretive dance during client meetings.

But hold on, it's not just about being a lovable weirdo. Your brand story needs to have depth, substance, and a clear vision for the future. Weave in the passions that drive you, the challenges you've overcome, and the dream of revolutionizing the Botpress automation situation. After all, what's a good story without a little drama and a whole lot of determination?

Remember, your brand story isn't just words on a page – it's the foundation upon which you'll build a loyal following of clients who are as invested in your success as you are. So, pour your heart and soul into it, sprinkle in a dash of quirkiness, and watch as your agency's brand becomes as irresistible as a freshly baked batch of homemade cookies.

Developing a Consistent Visual Identity

In the world of Botpress Automation, where innovation and creativity reign supreme, your visual identity is the sartorial equivalent of a perfectly tailored suit – it's the first thing that catches the eye and sets the tone for everything that follows.

But let's be real, designing a cohesive visual identity isn't exactly a walk in the park. It's like trying to herd a group of frenzied squirrels into a synchronized dance routine. But fear not, my entrepreneurial friends, for we have the secret to creating a visual identity that's as captivating as a velociraptor in a tutu.

Start by embracing the unexpected. Forget about the traditional "corporate" aesthetic and instead, let your freak flag fly. Maybe your logo is a playful amalgamation of Botpress icons and emojis, or perhaps your color palette is a delightful clash of neon hues that would make even the bravest of fashion icons do a double take.

And don't stop there – carry that rebellious spirit throughout every aspect of your visual brand, from your website design to your social media presence. Sprinkle in a few unexpected flourishes, like animated GIFs that capture the zany spirit of your agency or a branded merchandise line that features your team members dressed up as their favorite Botpress characters.

Remember, the key to a truly stand out visual identity is to create something that's so uniquely you that your clients can't help but be drawn in. So, embrace your inner weirdo, let your creativity run wild, and watch as your Botpress Automation Agency becomes the talk of the town – for all the right reasons.

Promoting Your Brand through Thought Leadership

In the ever evolving world of Botpress Automation, standing out from the crowd is no easy feat. But fear not, my friends, for we have the secret weapon to catapult your agency into the spotlight: thought leadership.

Now, I know what you're thinking – "Thought leadership? Isn't that just a fancy way of saying 'blah, blah, blah' on a bunch of online platforms?" Well, my dear entrepreneurs, you couldn't be more wrong. Thought leadership is the art of positioning yourself as an indispensable authority in your field, and it's the key to turning your Botpress Automation Agency into a must have service provider.

So, how do you become a influencer in the world of Botpress? It all starts with being a persistent knowledge seeker. Immerse yourself in the latest industry trends, dive deep into the intricacies of the Botpress platform, and explore the cutting edge applications of automation technology. Then, take that wealth of knowledge and transform it into a smorgasbord of captivating content that will have your clients and competitors alike clamoring for more.

But here's the kicker – don't just regurgitate dry, technical information. Infuse your thought leadership with a healthy dose of personality and a sprinkle of humor. After all, who wants to read yet another bland, corporate blog post when they could be learning about the latest Botpress hacks from a self proclaimed "automation ninja" who's not afraid to crack the occasional dad joke?

Employ a wide range of platforms to share your observations, from industry leading blogs and podcasts to social media platforms that allow you to showcase your unique brand of expertise. And don't be afraid to get a little creative – maybe you host a webinar series where you and your team dress up as famous Botpress characters, or you launch a video series where you solve real world automation challenges in a way that's as entertaining as it is informative.

Remember, the key to successful thought leadership is to consistently deliver value, build trust, and establish yourself as an indispensable resource in the world of Botpress Automation. So, embrace your inner weirdo, let your passion for all things Botpress shine, and watch as your agency becomes the go to authority in the industry.

Cultivating a Talented Team

Recruiting and Onboarding the Right Talent

Building a Botpress Automation Agency is no walk in the park, and you're going to need a crack team of mavericks to make it happen. Forget those cookie cutter resumes - we're talking about finding the type of people who can turn a simple chatbot into a riveting drama worthy of a Hollywood blockbuster. But how do you separate the coding ninjas from the keyboard smashing amateurs? It's all about embracing the chaos, my friend.

First and foremost, ditch the traditional job postings. Who has time to sift through a sea of generic cover letters when you could be out there scouring the dark corners of the internet for the true unicorns? Attend hackathons, meet ups, and underground bot fighting tournaments - that's where you'll find the real talent. Look for the ones with the glint in their eye, the ones who can turn a line of code into a symphony of unbridled creativity.

When it comes to the interview process, forget the stuffy, scripted questions. Instead, challenge your candidates to a good, old fashioned bot battle. Give them a random prompt, a tight deadline, and let the chaos unfold. The ones who emerge victorious, covered in virtual bot fuel and sporting the biggest, manic grins, those are your people. Hire them on the spot and watch as they transform your agency into a well oiled, Botpress wielding machine.

But the hiring process is just the beginning. Onboarding these mavericks requires a delicate touch, a dance of equal parts structure and spontaneity. Forget the generic employee handbooks and instead, craft a uniquely tailored "Chaos Survival Guide." Fill it with insider tips, like how to make the coffee machine do the robot, or the secret code to open up the hidden door that leads to the experimental bot lab. Make them feel like they're part of an elite, underground society of Botpress wizards, and they'll be loyal to you for life.

Promoting a Collaborative Work Culture

Now that you've assembled your crack team of Botpress ninjas, it's time to release their true potential. But here's the thing - these aren't your typical 9 to-5 desk jockeys. These are the kind of people who thrive on spontaneity, who see a problem and immediately start brainstorming ways to solve it with a complex web of bots and APIs. So, how do you use that boundless energy and creativity without turning your agency into a pure pandemonium?

It all starts with embracing the chaos. Forget about those stuffy, corporate team building exercises. Instead, host monthly bot building competitions, where your employees can showcase their skills and battle it out for the coveted "Bot iful" trophy. Encourage them to experiment, to push the boundaries of what's possible with Botpress. Who knows, that zany chatbot idea that sounds like it came straight from the mind of a sleep deprived mad scientist might just be the key to uncovering your next big client.

Speaking of clients, make sure your team is always in the loop. Regular "Botpress Briefings" are a must, where you can share the latest updates, discuss challenges, and brainstorm original solutions together. And don't be afraid to let your employees take the lead – after all, they're the ones who truly understand the ins and outs of your Botpress deployments. Authorize them to make decisions, to try new things, and to ultimately shape the direction of your agency.

Remember, a happy, engaged team is a productive team. So, be the kind of boss who's not afraid to don a funny hat and join in the bot dancing shenanigans. Show them that you're just as invested in the success of your agency as they are, and they'll have your back through thick and thin. Because let's face it, building a Botpress Automation Agency is no easy feat – but with the right team by your side, the possibilities are truly limitless.

Providing Ongoing Training and Development

In the ever evolving world of Botpress, standing still is the surest way to get left behind. That's why continuous learning and development are not just nice to-haves, but essential ingredients in the recipe for a thriving Botpress Automation Agency. After all, your team is the backbone of your business, and you need to make sure they're always one step ahead of the curve.

Start by creating a vigorous "Botpress Mastery" program, where your employees can dive deep into the latest platform updates, explore cutting edge features, and share their hard won perceptions with the rest of the team. Encourage them to attend industry events, participate in online forums, and even contribute to the Botpress community through tutorials and open source projects. The more they immerse themselves in the Botpress community, the more they'll become indispensable assets to your agency.

But it's not just about technical skills – you also need to nurture their soft skills, the ones that will help them excel in client facing roles and project management. Organize regular workshops on effective communication, creative problem solving, and the art of delivering exceptional customer service. After all, your Botpress experts might be coding wizards, but they also need to be able to translate their technical prowess into tangible business value for your clients.

And let's not forget about the importance of personal growth. Encourage your team to explore their passions and interests beyond the realm of Botpress. Sponsor them to attend conferences in related fields, like AI, machine learning, or even improv comedy (you never know when those skills might come in handy). By investing in their all-comprising development, you're not just helping them become better employees – you're shaping them into well rounded, new thinkers who can take your Botpress Automation Agency to new heights.

Leveraging Strategic Partnerships

Identifying Complementary Service Providers

In the dynamic world of Botpress automation, partnerships can be the secret sauce that takes your agency to the next level. But it's not just about finding any old collaborator - it's about carefully curating a network of complementary service providers who can improve your products and help you stand out in a crowded market.

Begin by conducting a thorough analysis of your current service suite. Where are your strengths? Where do you lack expertise or resources? These are the gaps you'll want to fill by seeking out strategic partners. Think beyond the obvious - sure, you might partner with a top notch Botpress developer, but what about a data visualization wizard who can bring your clients' analytics to life? Or a content marketing maven who can craft irresistible brand stories?

Networking is key here, but don't just attend the usual industry events. Get creative - attend local entrepreneurship meetups, join online communities, or even strike up conversations at the laundromat (you never know where you'll find your next big collaborator). The key is to keep your eyes peeled for service providers who share your values, your commitment to excellence, and your passion for pushing the boundaries of what's possible with Botpress.

Establishing Mutually Beneficial Partnerships

Once you've identified your dream partners, it's time to start building those relationships. And no, we're not talking about a simple "you scratch my back, I'll scratch yours" arrangement. True strategic partnerships are about creating a symbiotic community where everyone involved stands to gain.

Start by having open, honest conversations about your respective goals, strengths, and is an issue. What can you offer each other? How can you complement each other's services? Explore ways to create joint service services, share leads, or even co develop original Botpress solutions. The key is to find that sweet spot where your partnership not only benefits your clients but also drives growth and profitability for both of your businesses.

Don't be afraid to get creative with your partnership structures, either. Maybe it's a revenue sharing arrangement, a jointly owned intellectual property, or even an equity stake in each other's companies. The important thing is to ensure that the terms are fair, transparent, and synced with your shared vision for success.

Collaborating on Joint Projects

Now that you've laid the groundwork for your strategic partnerships, it's time to put them into action. Collaborating on joint projects is where the real magic happens – where you can use each other's expertise, resources, and networks to deliver truly remarkable results for your clients.

Start by identifying opportunities where your combined capabilities can create a compelling, one of-a kind solution. Maybe it's a complex Botpress deployment that requires specialized technical expertise and creative branding. Or perhaps it's a content marketing campaign that blends your partner's thought leadership with your agency's Botpress automation prowess.

Approach these joint projects with the same level of diligence and attention to detail as you would any other client engagement. Establish clear roles, responsibilities, and communication protocols. Develop a strong project management framework to ensure uninterrupted coordination and timely delivery. And most importantly, make sure that every decision and outcome matches with your shared vision for the project and your respective business goals.

By collaborating on high impact, high visibility projects, you'll not only deliver exceptional results for your clients but also solidify your partnerships as trusted, indispensable allies in the ever evolving world of Botpress automation.

Navigating Regulatory Compliance

Understanding Relevant Industry Regulations

As an automation agency, it's important to stay up to-date with the ever evolving situation of industry regulations. While the freedom of the digital realm may seem boundless, there are still critical rules and guidelines that must be adhered to, lest you find yourself in a tangled web of legal complications. Sure, you could take the "ignorance is bliss" approach, but trust me, that's a surefire way to end up in a world of hurt.

The first step is to dive deep into the specific regulations governing your clients' industries. Are you working with healthcare providers? Then you'll need to familiarize yourself with HIPAA compliance. Handling sensitive financial data? Brace yourself for the PCI DSS gauntlet. And don't even get me started on the convoluted web of privacy laws like GDPR and CCPA - they'll make your head spin faster than a Botpress bot on Red Bull.

But fear not, my fellow automation mavens! With a little elbow grease and a healthy dose of legal research, you can navigate these regulatory waters with the grace of a seasoned sailor. Stay vigilant, keep those compliance checklists handy, and never underestimate the power of a good lawyer on speed dial.

Implementing Vigorous Security and Privacy Measures

In the high stakes world of automation, security and privacy are no laughing matter. As the custodians of your clients' sensitive data and mission critical processes, you have a solemn responsibility to protect them against the ever evolving threats of the digital scene. Fail to do so, and you might as well be handing over the keys to the kingdom to a band of tech savvy cyber pirates.

Start by fortifying your Botpress deployments with industry standard security protocols. Encryption, access controls, and rigorous authentication procedures are the bare minimum. But don't stop there - explore into the latest advancements in AI powered threat detection, firewalls that could outsmart a grandmaster chess player, and backup systems so strong, they could survive a nuclear apocalypse.

Privacy is equally very important. Implement airtight data management policies, ensure compliance with relevant regulations, and consider deploying cutting edge anonymization techniques. After all, your clients' trust is the foundation of your success - and you can't afford to let a single byte of their information fall into the wrong hands.

Ensuring Ethical and Compliant Practices

In the fast paced world of automation, it's easy to get swept up in the race for efficiency and profits. But let's not forget the importance of maintaining the highest ethical standards.

After all, you're not just building bots - you're shaping the very fabric of your clients' businesses, and that comes with a great responsibility.

Start by establishing a vigorous code of conduct that clearly outlines your agency's values and principles. Transparency, honesty, and a commitment to social responsibility should be the cornerstones of your practices. Educate your team on the importance of ethical decision making, and allow them to speak up whenever they encounter a situation that might raise ethical red flags.

But it's not just about internal policies - you also need to ensure that your Botpress deployments are in line with industry proven methods and regulatory requirements. Implement rigorous testing protocols, continuously monitor for compliance, and be ready to adapt your solutions as the setting evolves. Because at the end of the day, your reputation is on the line, and the only thing worse than a bot that doesn't work is one that lands you in legal hot water.

Driving Sustainable Growth

Diversifying Your Revenue Streams

As your Botpress Automation Agency continues to thrive, it's essential to keep a keen eye on diversifying your revenue streams. Relying solely on a single income source can leave your business vulnerable to market shifts and unexpected disruptions. Instead, embrace a multi pronged approach that allows you to adapt and seize new opportunities as they arise.

Start by assessing your current service options and identifying complementary services that you can introduce. Perhaps you've been laser focused on building custom Botpress integrations, but there's a growing demand for chatbot maintenance and content curation. Expand your portfolio to cater to these emerging needs, and watch your revenue grow.

Another avenue to explore is leveraging your Botpress expertise beyond client work. Consider offering training programs, online courses, or even developing and selling your own Botpress based tools and templates. By monetizing your knowledge and intellectual property, you create a sustainable income stream that can provide a buffer against fluctuations in your client facing services.

Don't be afraid to venture into adjacent industries, either. Your Botpress skills and experience can be valuable in a wide range of sectors, from e commerce and healthcare to finance and education. Diversify your client base and tap into new markets to open up a world of revenue generating opportunities.

As you explore these new revenue streams, remember to maintain a sharp focus on quality and customer satisfaction. Your reputation and the trust you've built with your existing clients will be the foundation for your continued success. Strive to deliver exceptional service and value in everything you do, and your business will reap the rewards.

Exploring International Expansion Opportunities

With the rise of remote work and the global nature of the digital terrain, it's time to start thinking beyond your local or national borders. Exploring international expansion opportunities can open up a world of possibilities for your Botpress Automation Agency.

Begin by researching potential markets that harmonize with your service services and expertise. Look for regions with a growing demand for Botpress powered solutions, a receptive client base, and a favorable business climate. Consider factors like regulatory environments, language barriers, and cultural nuances that may impact your expansion strategy.

Once you've identified promising markets, develop a tailored approach to enter these new territories. This may involve establishing a local presence, partnering with regional distribution channels, or even setting up a remote team to serve international clients. Employ digital tools and platforms to rationalize your operations and deliver your services across borders.

Navigating the complexities of international expansion can be daunting, but it's a surefire way to make accessible exponential growth. Embrace the challenge and see it as an opportunity to diversify your client base, tap into new revenue streams, and establish your Botpress Automation Agency as a global leader in the field.

Remember, successful international expansion is not a one size-fits all proposition. Remain responsive, adaptable, and open to learning as you venture into new markets. Regularly review your strategy, gather feedback from your international clients, and continuously refine your approach to ensure long term success.

Implementing Data Driven Decision Making

In the fast paced world of Botpress Automation, data is the lifeblood of your business. By embracing a data driven approach to decision making, you can propel your agency to new heights of success and ensure the long term sustainability of your growth.

Start by establishing a powerful data collection and analysis infrastructure. Apply the wealth of metrics and analytics available through your Botpress deployments, website analytics, and customer relationship management (CRM) tools. Identify the key performance indicators (KPIs) that matter most to your business, and meticulously track and analyze this data.

But don't stop at just collecting the numbers. Dive deep into the realizations hidden within the data, looking for patterns, trends, and opportunities for optimization. Use these perceptions to inform your strategic decision making, from refining your service selections and pricing models to optimizing your marketing campaigns and client onboarding processes.

Equip your team to embrace a data driven mindset as well. Encourage them to contribute their own observations and recommendations, encouraging a culture of continuous improvement and innovation. Regularly review your data and metrics together, and collaborate on developing practical plans to address any is a difficulty or areas for growth.

As your Botpress Automation Agency matures, consider investing in advanced data analytics tools and techniques. Use the power of machine learning, predictive modeling, and business intelligence to uncover hidden realizations and make more informed, data driven decisions. This commitment to data driven excellence will set your agency apart from the competition and solidify your position as a trusted partner for your clients.

Leaving a Lasting Legacy

Giving Back to the Community

As your Botpress Automation Agency continues to thrive, it's important to remember the significance of giving back to the community that has supported your journey. After all, the true mark of a successful entrepreneur is not just the wealth they've amassed, but the positive impact they've made on the world around them.

One of the most rewarding ways to leave a lasting legacy is through philanthropic initiatives. Consider establishing a charitable foundation or partnering with local non profits to support causes that sync with your values. Whether it's funding STEM education programs, providing job training for underprivileged youth, or supporting environmental conservation efforts, your contributions can make a tangible difference in the lives of those who need it most.

But philanthropy doesn't have to be limited to monetary donations. Encourage your team to volunteer their time and expertise to local organizations, encouraging a culture of community engagement and social responsibility within your agency. Organizing regular volunteering events or offering paid time off for employees to give back can inspire your staff and strengthen your brand's reputation as a socially conscious and purpose driven business.

Remember, your legacy is not just about the financial success of your Botpress Automation Agency - it's about the positive ripple effects you can create in the world. By embedding a spirit of generosity and civic mindedness into the core of your business, you'll leave an indelible mark that extends far beyond the bottom line.

Mentoring and Allowing Future Entrepreneurs

As an established Botpress Automation Agency, you've undoubtedly faced your fair share of challenges and overcome numerous obstacles on the path to success. Now, it's time to pay it forward and allow the next generation of entrepreneurs.

Consider launching a mentorship program within your agency, where seasoned members of your team can share their observations and experiences with aspiring business owners. These one on-one or group mentorship sessions can cover a wide range of topics, from navigating the complexities of Botpress deployment to developing effective marketing strategies and cultivating a thriving company culture.

But your mentorship efforts don't have to be limited to your immediate network. Reach out to local universities, incubators, or entrepreneurial hubs and offer to host workshops, guest lectures, or office hours to share your expertise with a broader audience. By inspiring and enabling the next wave of innovators, you'll not only be shaping the future of the Botpress industry, but you'll also be carving out a legacy as a respected expert and community builder.

Remember, the true mark of a successful entrepreneur is not just the wealth they've amassed, but the knowledge and wisdom they've imparted to those who follow in their footsteps. By mentoring and supporting the growth of aspiring business owners, you'll be creating a ripple effect that extends far beyond the walls of your Botpress Automation Agency, and solidifying your place as a true pillar of the entrepreneurial network.

Reflecting on Your Entrepreneurial Journey

As you look back on the incredible journey that has led you to this point, it's important to take the time to reflect on the lessons learned, the challenges overcome, and the milestones achieved. After all, your entrepreneurial story is not just a tale of business success – it's a evidence to the power of perseverance, innovation, and unwavering determination.

Consider documenting your entrepreneurial journey through a memoir, a series of blog posts, or even a podcast. Sharing your personal experiences, the crucial moments that shaped your vision, and the strategies that led to your agency's growth can inspire and allow others who are starting on their own entrepreneurial paths.

Reflect on the crucial decisions you made, the risks you took, and the lessons you learned along the way. How did you overcome the initial challenges of building a Botpress Automation Agency from scratch? What were the key turning points that propelled your business to new heights? By opening up about your triumphs and setbacks, you'll not only solidify your legacy as a successful entrepreneur, but you'll also provide a roadmap for others to follow in your footsteps.

As you look towards the future, remember that your entrepreneurial journey is far from over. Continue to seek out new opportunities for growth, innovation, and personal development. Stay curious, embrace change, and never stop learning. By doing so, you'll not only keep your Botpress Automation Agency at the forefront of the industry, but you'll also inspire countless others to pursue their own entrepreneurial dreams.

Silas Meadowlark

www.ingramcontent.com/pod-product-compliance
Lightning Source LLC
Chambersburg PA
CBHW030031250526
45464CB00026B/2660